RED DOT

An Inspirational Short Story about a Remarkable Dog and the Children He Loved

Bettie J. Burres

Copyright © 2013 by Bettie J. Burres

All rights reserved, including the right to reproduce this work in any form whatsoever, without permission in writing from the publisher, except for brief passages in connection with a review.

Publisher: Bettie Young Book Publishers

Bettie Youngs Books are distributed worldwide. If you are unable to order this book from your local bookseller, Espresso, or online, you may order directly from the publisher.

BETTIE YOUNGS BOOK PUBLISHERS
www.BettieYoungsBooks.com
info@BettieYoungsBooks.com

ISBN: 978-1-936332-66-3
eBook: 978-1-936332-73-1

Library of Congress Control Number: 2012948065

1. Bettie Youngs Books. 2. Burres, Bettie J. 3. Farm Life. 4. Growing Up. 5. Inspiration. 6. Pets. 7. Family Life. 8. Border Collie. 9. Dogs.

Printed in the United States of America

RED DOT

We were four spirited little children in motion, prancing around in circles, poking, pinching, playfully slapping each other, giggling and squealing, burning up the last bits of seemingly infinite energy before bedtime—or so our mother hoped. Unexpectedly, the house lights went out, followed by our mother's sudden and abrupt order: "Shh!"

Just as a baby animal knows its mother's call, we knew precisely how to decipher the meaning behind our mother's tone of voice. Like a science, we knew when "Shh" held the possibility of a hug or the possibility of a spanking. "Shh" was the tone of alarm, immediacy.

Eight little eyes searched our mother's eyes for clues. Sensing uncertainty in her voice and anxiety in her eyes, we felt her fear and obeyed her orders. Frightened of whatever had alarmed our mother, we stood motionless and silent in the middle of the floor, peering through the darkness to keep her silhouette in sight. Mother quietly glided to the kitchen window and stared through the blinds in the direction of the red dot coming down the lane.

Curious, I whispered, "What do you see?"

"A red dot," was her answer.

"Will it kill us?" asked my little brother. Alarmed, he sucked on his thumb frantically.

"No, no, it won't hurt us," Mom whispered, but her voice undermined the veil of bravery she wore for the sake of her children. Unconvinced, four little bodies scampered under the kitchen table, inching and nudging closer together, as though huddling would somehow guarantee their safety. "If we're quiet, it'll go away," my older sister reassured us. She wanted to believe—as did the rest of us—that our stillness would protect us and banish our mother's fear.

Ever so silently, our mother peeked through the blinds again for a better glimpse at the thing coming up the lane, searching the darkness for the red dot that frightened her so.

This was not the first time our mother had witnessed an encroacher, nor the first time she'd gathered her children and stood watch over them. On nights when my father worked late in the fields harvesting the crops, I'd heard my mother tell him about this thing. Dad had dealings with the red dot, too. On several occasions, he took down the trusty old Winchester and shot into the air as a warning. That was usually enough.

How I wished Dad were here now. Our mother wouldn't be fearful then, and we wouldn't be hovering in the dark. But Dad wouldn't come to our rescue tonight; he'd gone to buy livestock at an auction nearly 200 miles away and wouldn't be back until early morning. Tonight, my mother faced the intruder with four small children at her side.

As was the case in rural life, a thief would sometimes come onto farms in the late dark of the night to loot a shed, or steal a chicken or goose. Gas was the most valued commodity, though shovels, axes, machine tools, and even livestock sometimes disappeared.

"Stay under the table, kids, and be very quiet," our mother warned. Our collie, Teddy, was on the porch, aware that something wasn't quite right. His gentle brown eyes were framed by an enormous head and his body covered with a beautiful chocolate, yellow, and white mane. Sensing trouble, Teddy looked at Mom through the window for instructions: should he lay low or begin a crusade of barking?

My mother looked from Teddy to the shadows of her four children and back to the dog. He understood perfectly: he would be silent for now. With vigilant ears pointed in the air, Teddy crouched and rested his head on outstretched paws, continuing to watch the lane. Attentive and heedful, his energized body was ready for action. The Burres clan was his family, and he was guarding it.

Teddy had come to our family by way of Christmas stocking when he was six weeks old. We were a smaller family then, just two adults and two little, curly-headed, freckled-faced girls. He'd been with us nearly six years now and had watched the family grow larger and noisier with the birth of each new child. Giving and accepting love was a big job, but he was up to it. There was never a dull moment for him. He helped Dad corral the livestock in the morning and bring the cows home each evening. He walked the older children to the bus and pined until their return. Mom always called him to walk with her down the lane to get the mail. When she went to town, he knew he was expected to sit on the front porch by the door and guard the house.

Some of us needed him more than others. When the smallest of the children cried, when the oldest left for school, Teddy was a comfort and a pillow to curl up with. When my mother reached for a washcloth to wash the baby's face, Teddy licked the child's face to save her a trip. He knew everyone's quirks and loved each of us all the more.

He knew how to play us to get what he wanted, too. As the sun began its rise or set, wonderful aromas poured from the house, and he would check the old screen door. A wooden clothespin wedged at the bottom meant that four kids were about to become accomplices to his hideout under the kitchen table. Mom forbade animals in the house, even if they were members of the family. With a paw or nose, he would slyly open the screen, watch carefully for Mom to turn her back, and dash under the table where he hid illegally and was fed illegally, too.

When we children were put to bed, he'd sit beneath our window and whimper softly until we opened it, removed the screen, and hoisted him up and into our bedroom by head, hair, or leg. No matter how much pain we lovingly inflicted, he endured it, gladly. And he was smart. He knew when the footsteps coming down the hall belonged to Mom or to Dad, and knew exactly what to do when one of us children hissed, "Go!" That meant he was to disappear under the bed and lie there silently until the big pair of feet left the room. He knew "It's clear!" meant it was safe to come out. Content with his leadership role by day, he didn't mind being our puppet by night.

Red Dot

"What is the red dot, Mama?" one little brother wanted to know.

"Please tell us," the rest of us begged.

"It's a man smoking a cigarette, walking up our lane," she whispered.

"Let Teddy get him," one brother said, with an air of confidence. "He'll chase him away!" Hearing our voices, Teddy slid closer to the window, ready to pounce on command.

"No, he may hurt Teddy," replied Mom.

"Nobody would kill Teddy," my sister countered matter-of-factly, as though saying so was built-in protection. My two brothers and I nodded our heads in agreement. It was unthinkable that anyone could entertain a bad thought about our prized playmate, who had rescued our brother three days before when we children had been down at the stream panning for crawdads.

Teddy would be needed tonight. With everyone tense and fearful, the whole family was on alert. He looked at Mom's face to get a read on her emotions, to see if anything had changed.

"Shhh!" Mom whispered, her eyes following the ever-so-close red dot.

"It is a bad man!" shrieked my older sister in disbelief, seeing the red dot emerge from the darkness.

Red Dot

Red Dot was now at the mouth of the lane, where house, sheds, and barnyards were positioned in a circle on four acres of homestead. The moonlight was bright, and we could now see him more clearly. He was tall and slender, wearing faded, tattered jeans and a dark T-shirt. His sleeves were rolled up, displaying a length of a thin arm, making it obvious to me that Dad was stronger than he was. His jeans rode up over laced-up, high-top boots.

Red Dot dropped his cigarette to the ground and ground it out with his boot. He looked first in the direction of the house and then to the farm sheds nearby. Next he began walking in the direction of the house. Changing his mind, he turned and walked toward the sheds. He strolled over to the small machine shed that doubled as garage for Dad's truck, peered in the window, and moved hastily to the door. We saw him reach into his back pocket for a tool and remove the hinge in minutes.

The cows and their young calves in the yards nearby stood watching, no longer chewing their cuds as they do when content. Noting the animals had fallen silent, Red Dot threw the hinge and dangling lock in the cattle's direction. They hit the fence and fell to the ground with a thud. The seven wild Canadian geese, their wings clipped so they wouldn't fly away, scattered and honked in protest. Their sleep had been disturbed. Their loud cackling started a chain reaction of nervous alert signals from all the animals on the homestead: the ducks quacked, chickens clucked, pigs snorted, lambs bleated, mother cows bellowed to their calves, and the horses—equally nervous—strode aimlessly around their pen. The ruckus caused Red Dot to step into the shadow of the gap pump nearby. His body faded from our sight.

He needn't have worried. No shots would be fired tonight.

Long moments passed.

Perhaps reassured that no one was home—farm lights had not come on and there was no car in the garage—Red Dot's body language changed. He no longer walked quickly with his flashlight off. He sidled over to the garage and stepped in, letting the door slam behind him. The beam of his flashlight darted up and down and side-to-side, no doubt inventorying the contents. He emerged clutching a burlap gunnysack, the kind issued to farmers when their seed corn and seed beans orders were filled in the spring. "RESERVED FOR BURRES" was stamped in bold black letters on our bags.

Red Dot then ambled over to the large machine shed where Dad kept his machine tools and machinery. He'd purchased them second-hand at farm sales or acquired them in a trade with a neighbor. After several attempts to break the chain, Red Dot threw his tall, skinny frame against the double door. He was too light to cave in the door, but he made a thunderous rolling sound. Mom yanked my sister and me flat to the floor, and Teddy stared at Mom, waiting for her to say "Sic 'em!"

A choir of noise erupted from the menagerie of animals again, but Red Dot ignored them. He took his flashlight and, with one quick blow, broke the window. He dumped out the lumpy burlap seed sack, wrenches and tools clanging as they fell to the ground. Red Dot then took a bale from the nearby stack, placed it beneath the broken window and stepped up. He wrapped his gloved hands with the burlap bag, no doubt to protect himself from the jagged chips of glass that remained in the window sill. With that, he hoisted himself up on the sill, inching his body through the window.

He was in the shed a very long time. When he finally emerged, Red Dot walked to the gas pump and studied its lock. He appeared to count off the paces to the underground storage unit that held hundreds of gallons of gas; then he disappeared into the livestock yard where the head of cattle masked his progress. The moon no longer cast a luminescent glow, and it was too dark to follow his path, impossible to see what he was doing.

We were unaware that Red Dot was making his way to the house.

But Teddy knew.

Without warning, the dog slithered off the porch and crouched in the yard, where he continued to observe the stalker's every move.

"Teddy!" my mother quietly called to the dog. "Get back here!" He tilted his head slightly in her direction and defied her order. He knew what he needed to do more than she did. No one dared come near his family, and that included Red Dot. Belly dragging on the ground, Teddy crawled across the length of the yard toward the large wooden sandbox Dad had built for us. Teddy crouched beside it and continued his observation in secrecy.

Heavy footsteps thudded on the porch. They were Red Dot's. Teddy let out a low, belly-wrenching howl, moving his head up and to the side to throw his voice, like a ventriloquist. It worked. Red Dot, his body now tense, cautiously stepped down from the porch and walked into the yard, trying to assess the curious sound he'd heard.

Continuing his ploy to draw the man toward him and away from the house, Teddy made a series of other weird sounds. As Red Dot walked toward the noise, Teddy, with his body flat against the ground, backed away from the sandbox and disappeared into the darkness. Red Dot shook his head, like he was hearing imaginary sounds.

Seemingly confounded, he approached the porch once again. From somewhere in the blackness, Teddy let out the strangest and most bloodcurdling sound I'd ever heard from an animal.

Startled, Red Dot turned back toward the sound, scanning the darkness. Obviously fearful, he reached into the burlap bag and pulled out my father's long, shiny metal wrench. He dropped the sack of stolen goods and walked slowly toward the middle of the yard, holding the wrench in front of himself as protection.

Teddy had him where he wanted him. He'd circled Red Dot and now inched toward the man, slithering silently up behind him. We all watched as our dog, our gentle companion, stiffened his body and bared his teeth. Then he struck.

Teddy threw himself at Red Dot with such force that the man instantly fell to the ground. Red Dot rolled over and tried to get to his feet. But Teddy attacked him again, growling and barking as he protected his family. Swearing profusely now, Red Dot staggered to his feet, his left arm bloody and dangling to his side.

Teddy struck again. But he was outmanned by Red Dot, who raised his hand and with furious force struck our magnificent dog in the head with the steel wrench. Crying and yelping in pain, Teddy crashed to the ground.

Teddy! We knew our guardian angel was now badly injured.

Determined to get the better of Red Dot, Teddy rose up, mentally numb to his injured body. The man didn't recognize this magnificent animal as a kindred spirit as well as a warrior, and he slammed the wrench at our pet again and again and again.

"Nooo!" screamed Judy. "Don't hurt Teddy!"

"He's our doggie. Don't hurt our doggie," Mark cried in anguish, tears running down his face. The littlest child screamed and cried in unison with his brother and sisters. All four children dashed to the door.

Mother rushed to guard the door, trying to stop her children from going to Teddy's rescue. "Let us out, let us out!" we screamed, seeing Mother as the enemy trying to prevent us from running to help our Teddy. Four children rioted and ran into the yard to take care of Teddy the way he had taken care of us so many times.

Teddy was on the ground, soaked in his own blood. The dog we loved with so much passion lay moaning and gasping for air. Slowly, he lifted his head to see us.

"It's okay," soothed my sister. "We won't let him hurt you again." Tears streamed from her face onto Teddy's fur. I stroked his broken and bloody body, trying to send him all the love and compassion I felt for him. He looked at me sadly and jerked as pain seared through his body. I held him tightly, hoping my strength would emanate from my body and transfer to his.

But we were too late. The last breath had seeped from his body. Our Teddy didn't move again.

Perhaps because Red Dot heard us crying and watched as we caressed our dying dog, or perhaps because he saw Teddy turn his head toward the house to notify our mother she must take over from here, the man must have felt the bond between the dog and his family. I like to think that in those last moments Red Dot felt a touch of remorse over killing such a beautiful animal, an animal justified in attacking him.

Whatever it was, Red Dot hurriedly limped away, taking the sack of stolen items with him.

It's hard to comfort children when they have witnessed a brutal attack on their pet, especially one that was as much a part of them as Teddy had been. One by one, we children sought solace in our mother's arms. She held and rocked us, too overcome herself by grief to say anything, knowing her children had lost their innocence as well as their beloved dog.

We always remembered Teddy and included him in our play for a year after he was killed. In spirit, Teddy

Red Dot

joined us children for baseball games: "Catch one for Teddy!" Kevin would say, paying homage to the dog that had tolerated our antics and loved us so.

* * *

On a Sunday afternoon about six months later, a red pickup pulled into our farmyard and a tall, slender, rather handsome man emerged. He said he was from Fort Dodge, about fifteen miles away, and was here visiting friends. "Say," he said speaking to my father, "I still have one puppy left from a large litter, and I thought I might get lucky and find him a home. I thought with your large yard and all these kids, you might want him. Every child should have a dog, don't you think?"

The man talked fast and looked over his shoulder nervously.

"I have the pup in the truck. If it's okay with you, I'll show him to the kids and see whether they like him." He looked at my father, saw no resistance and hurried to his pickup. Four very excited children followed him. He opened the passenger door of his truck and lifted a small, plump, clean-smelling collie pup out of a cardboard box. Within seconds, we were all stroking and petting him, talking to him and arguing over whose turn it was to hold him next. Our hearts were smitten.

Red Dot

With one voice, we called to our parents. "Can we keep him, please? Please? Please?" We offered all the bargains children do, swearing to feed and care for the puppy ourselves, to do all our chores, to go to bed without complaining, and a million and one other things designed to soften parents' hearts.

Dad looked the stranger over. "Looks like a nice collie pup. Why aren't you selling him? You could probably get a good price for a fine dog like that."

We children looked up, terror-stricken that the stranger would change his mind and take the dog away from us. Judy, who was holding the puppy at the time, hugged him so hard he let out a yelp. The stranger smiled at us and pulled out a cigarette. Lighting it, he said, "No, no . . . you folks would be doing me a favor, put my mind at rest, if you'd take the dog. I just want him to have a good home. And like I said, kids should have a dog. Lotta love between kids and dogs, you know." Chuckling, he added, "It looks like they like him all right."

Mom and Dad exchanged glances, but it was clear that they'd already given in. "Okay, Mister, and thanks," Dad told him. "It looks as if the kids have a new dog. Since he's just a pup, guess we'd better take his box, too."

Red Dot

I ran back to retrieve the box. That's when I saw the rumpled burlap bag. It was marked "Reserved for Burres."

Red Dot had come back to repay a debt.

Other Books by Bettie Youngs Book Publishers

On Toby's Terms

Charmaine Hammond

On Toby's Terms is an endearing story of a beguiling creature who teaches his owners that, despite their trying to teach him how to be the dog they want, he is the one to lay out the terms of being the dog he needs to be. This insight would change their lives forever.

"Simply a beautiful book about life, love, and purpose."
—**Jack Canfield, compiler,** *Chicken Soup for the Soul* **series**

"In a perfect world, every dog would have a home and every home would have a dog like Toby!" —**Nina Siemaszko, actress,** *The West Wing*

"This is a captivating, heartwarming story and we are very excited about bringing it to film." —**Steve Hudis, Producer**

ISBN: 978-0-9843081-4-9 • ePub: 978-1-936332-15-1 • $15.95

The Maybelline Story

And the Spirited Family Dynasty Behind It

Sharrie Williams

Throughout the twentieth century, Maybelline inflated, collapsed, endured, and thrived in tandem with the nation's upheavals. Williams, to avoid unwanted scrutiny of his private life, cloistered himself behind the gates of his Rudolph Valentino Villa and ran his empire from a distance. This never before told story celebrates the life of a man whose vision rocketed him to success along with the woman held in his orbit: his brother's wife, Evelyn Boecher—who became his lifelong fascination and muse. A fascinating and inspiring story, a tale both epic and intimate, alive with the clash, the hustle, the music, and dance of American enterprise.

"A richly told story of a forty-year, white-hot love triangle that fans the flames of a major worldwide conglomerate."
—**Neil Shulman, Associate Producer,** *Doc Hollywood*

"Salacious! Engrossing! There are certain stories, so dramatic, so sordid, that they seem positively destined for film; this is one of them." —*New York Post*

ISBN: 978-0-9843081-1-8 • ePub: 978-1-936332-17-15 • $18.95

It Started with Dracula

The Count, My Mother, and Me

Jane Congdon

The terrifying legend of Count Dracula silently skulking through the Transylvania night may have terrified generations of filmgoers, but the tall, elegant vampire captivated and electrified a young Jane Congdon, igniting a dream to one day see his mysterious land of ancient castles and misty hollows. Four decades later she finally takes her long-awaited trip—never dreaming that it would unearth decades-buried memories, and trigger a life-changing inner journey. A memoir full of surprises, Jane's story is one of hope, love—and second chances.

"Unfinished business can surface when we least expect it. *It Started with Dracula* is the inspiring story of two parallel journeys: one a carefully planned vacation and the other an astonishing and unexpected detour in healing a wounded heart."
  —**Charles Whitfield, MD, bestselling author of** *Healing the Child Within*

"An elegantly written and cleverly told story. An electrifying read."
  —**Diane Bruno, CISION Media**

ISBN: 978-1-936332-10-6 • ePub: 978-1-936332-11-3 • $15.95

The Rebirth of Suzzan Blac

Suzzan Blac

A horrific upbringing and then abduction into the sex slave industry would all but kill Suzzan's spirit to live. But a happy marriage and two children brought love—and forty-two stunning paintings, art so raw that it initially frightened even the artist. "I hid the pieces for 15 years," says Suzzan, "but just as with the secrets in this book, I am slowing sneaking them out, one by one by one." Now a renowned artist, her work is exhibited world-wide.

A story of inspiration, truth and victory.

"A solid memoir about a life reconstructed. Chilling, thrilling, and thought provoking."
  —**Pearry Teo, Producer,** *The Gene Generation*

ISBN: 978-1-936332-22-9 • ePub: 978-1-936332-23-6 • $16.95

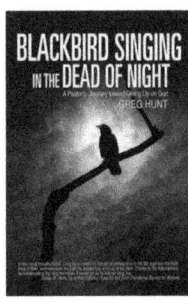

Blackbird Singing in the Dead of Night

What to Do When God Won't Answer

Gregory L. Hunt

Pastor Greg Hunt had devoted nearly thirty years to congregational ministry, helping people experience God and find their way in life. Then came his own crisis of faith and calling. While turning to God for guidance, he finds nothing. Neither his education nor his religious involvements could prepare him for the disorienting impact of the experience.

Alarmed, he tries an experiment. The result is startling—and changes his life entirely.

"In this most beautiful memoir, Greg Hunt invites us into an unsettling time in his life, exposes the fault lines of his faith, and describes the path he walked into and out of the dark. Thanks to the trail markers he leaves along the way, he makes it easier for us to find our way, too."
—**Susan M. Heim**, co-author, *Chicken Soup for the Soul, Devotional Stories for Women*

"Compelling. If you have ever longed to hear God whispering a love song into your life, read this book."
—**Gary Chapman**, *NY Times* **bestselling author,** *The Love Languages of God*

ISBN: 978-1-936332-07-6 • ePub: 978-1-936332-18-2 • $15.95

DON CARINA

WWII Mafia Heroine

Ron Russell

A father's death in Southern Italy in the 1930s—a place where women who can read are considered unfit for marriage—thrusts seventeen-year-old Carina into servitude as a "black widow," a legal head of the household who cares for her twelve siblings. A scandal forces her into a marriage to Russo, the "Prince of Naples."

By cunning force, Carina seizes control of Russo's organization and disguising herself as a man, controls the most powerful of Mafia groups for nearly a decade. Discovery is inevitable: Interpol has been watching. Nevertheless, Carina survives to tell her children her stunning story of strength and survival.

ISBN: 978-0-9843081-9-4 • ePub: 978-1-936332-49-6 • $15.95

Living with Multiple Personalities

The Christine Ducommun Story

Christine Ducommun

Christine Ducommun was a happily married wife and mother of two, when—after moving back into her childhood home—she began to experience panic attacks and a series of bizarre flashbacks. Eventually diagnosed with Dissociative Identity Disorder (DID), Christine's story details an extraordinary twelve-year ordeal unraveling the buried trauma of her past and the daunting path she must take to heal from it. Therapy helps to identify Christine's personalities and understand how each helped her cope with her childhood, but she'll need to understand their influence on her adult life. Fully reawakened and present, the personalities compete for control of Christine's mind as she bravely struggles to maintain a stable home for her growing children. In the shadows, her life tailspins into unimaginable chaos—bouts of drinking and drug abuse, sexual escapades, theft and fraud—leaving her to believe she may very well be losing the battle for her sanity. Nearing the point of surrender, a breakthrough brings integration.

A brave story of identity, hope, healing and love.

"Reminiscent of the Academy Award-winning *A Beautiful Mind,* this true story will have you on the edge of your seat. Spellbinding!"   **—Josh Miller, Producer**

ISBN: 978-0-9843081-5-6 • ePub: 978-1-936332-06-9 • $16.95

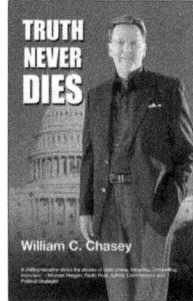

Truth Never Dies

William C. Chasey

A lobbyist for some 40 years, William C. Chasey represented some of the world's most prestigious business clients and twenty-three foreign governments before the US Congress. His integrity never questioned.

All that changed when Chasey was hired to forge communications between Libya and the US Congress. A trip he took with a US Congressman for discussions with then Libyan leader Muammar Qadhafi forever changed Chasey's life. Upon his return, his bank accounts were frozen, clients and friends had been advised not to take his calls.

Things got worse: the CIA, FBI, IRS, and the Federal Judiciary attempted to coerce him into using his unique Libyan access to participate in a CIA-sponsored assassination plot of the two Libyans indicted for the bombing of Pan Am flight 103. Chasey's refusal to cooperate resulted in the destruction of his reputation, a six-year FBI investigation and sting operation, financial ruin, criminal charges, and incarceration in federal prison.

"A somber tale, a thrilling read."   **—Gary Chafetz, author,** *The Perfect Villain*

ISBN: 978-1-936332-46-5 • ePub: 978-1-936332-47-2 • $24.95

Out of the Transylvania Night

Aura Imbarus

A Pulitzer-Prize entry

"I'd grown up in the land of Transylvania, homeland to Dracula, Vlad the Impaler, and worse, dictator Nicolae Ceausescu," writes the author. "Under his rule, like vampires, we came to life after sundown, hiding our heirloom jewels and documents deep in the earth." Fleeing to the US to rebuild her life, she discovers a startling truth about straddling two cultures and striking a balance between one's dreams and the sacrifices that allow a sense of "home."

"Aura's courage shows the degree to which we are all willing to live lives centered on freedom, hope, and an authentic sense of self. Truly a love story!"
—**Nadia Comaneci, Olympic Champion**

"A stunning account of erasing a past, but not an identity."
—**Todd Greenfield, 20th Century Fox**

ISBN: 978-0-9843081-2-5 • ePub:978-1-936332-20-5 • $14.95

Hostage of Paradox: A Memoir

John Rixey Moore

Few people then or now know about the clandestine war that the CIA ran in Vietnam, using the Green Berets for secret operations throughout Southeast Asia. This was not the Vietnam War of the newsreels, the body counts, rice paddy footage, and men smoking cigarettes on the sandbag bunkers. This was a shadow directive of deep-penetration interdiction, reconnaissance, and assassination missions conducted by a selected few Special Forces teams, usually consisting of only two Americans and a handful of Chinese mercenaries, called Nungs. These specialized units deployed quietly from forward operations bases to prowl through agendas that, for security reasons, were seldom completely understood by the men themselves.

Hostage of Paradox is the first-hand account by one of these elite team leaders.

"A compelling story told with extraordinary insight, disconcerting reality, and engaging humor."   —**David Hadley, actor,** *China Beach*

ISBN: 978-1-936332-37-3 • ePub: 978-1-936332-33-5 • $24.95

Crashers

A Tale of "Cappers" and "Hammers"

Lindy S. Hudis

The illegal business of fraudulent car accidents is a multi-million dollar racket, involving unscrupulous medical providers, personal injury attorneys, and the cooperating passengers involved in the accidents. Innocent people are often swept into it. Newly engaged Nathan and Shari, who are swimming in mounting debt, were easy prey: seduced by an offer from a stranger to move from hard times to good times in no time, Shari finds herself the "victim" in a staged auto accident. Shari gets her payday, but breaking free of this dark underworld will take nothing short of a miracle.

"A riveting story of love, life—and limits. A non-stop thrill ride."
—**Dennis "Danger" Madalone, stunt coordinator,** *Castle*

ISBN: 978-1-936332-27-4 • ePub: 978-1-936332-28-1 • $16.95

A World Torn Asunder

The Life and Triumph of Constantin C. Giurescu

Marina Giurescu, M.D.

Constantin C. Giurescu was Romania's leading historian and author of the seminal The History of the Romanian People. His granddaughter's fascinating story of this remarkable man and his family follows their struggles in war-torn Romania from 1900 to the fall of the Soviet Union. An "enlightened" society is dismantled with the 1946 Communist takeover of Romania, and Constantin is confined to the notorious Sighet penitentiary. Drawing on her grandfather's prison diary (which was put in a glass jar, buried in a yard, then smuggled out of the country by Dr. Paul E. Michelson—who does the FOREWORD for this book), private letters and her own research, Dr. Giurescu writes of the legacy from the turn of the century to the fall of Communism. We see the rise of modern Romania, the misery of World War I, the blossoming of its culture between the wars, and then the sellout of Eastern Europe to Russia after World War II. In this sweeping account, we see not only its effects socially and culturally, but the triumph in its wake: a man and his people who reclaim better lives for themselves, and in the process, teach us a lesson in endurance, patience, and will—not only to survive, but to thrive. Author Marina Giurescu, M.D. defected from Communist Romania and immigrated to the US in 1984 and is an MD working in the US.

"The inspirational story of a quiet man and his silent defiance in the face of tyranny."
—**Dr. Connie Mariano, author of** *The White House Doctor*

ISBN: 978-1-936332-76-2 • ePub: 978-1-936332-77-9 • $21.95

Trafficking the Good Life

Jennifer Myers

Jennifer Myers had worked long and hard toward a successful career as a dancer in Chicago, but just as her star was rising, she fell in love with the kingpin of a drug trafficking operation. Drawn to his life of luxury, she soon became a vital partner in driving marijuana across the country, making unbelievable sums of easy money that she stacked in shoeboxes and spent like an heiress.

Steeped in moral ambiguity, she sought to cleanse her soul with the guidance of spiritual gurus and New Age prophets—to no avail. Only time in a federal prison made her face up to and understand her choices. It was there, at rock bottom, that she discovered that her real prison was the one she had unwittingly made inside herself and where she could start rebuilding a life of purpose and ethical pursuit.

"A gripping memoir. When the DEA finally knocks on Myers's door, she and the reader both see the moment for what it truly is—not so much an arrest as a rescue."
—**Tony D'Souza, author of** *Whiteman and Mule*

"A stunningly honest exploration of a woman finding her way through a very masculine world . . . and finding her voice by facing the choices she has made."
—**Dr. Linda Savage, author of** *Reclaiming Goddess Sexuality*

ISBN: 978-1-936332-67-0 • ePub: 978-1-936332-68-7 • $18.95

The Law of Attraction for Teens

How to Get More of the Good Stuff, and Get Rid of the Bad Stuff!

Christopher Combates

Whether it's getting better grades, creating better relationships with your friends, parents, or teachers, or getting a date for the prom, the Law of Attraction just might help you bring it about. It works like this: Like attracts like. When we align our goals with our best intentions and highest purpose, when we focus on what we want, we are more likely to bring it about. This book will help teens learn how to think, act, and communicate in the positive way.

ISBN: 978-1-936332-29-8 • ePub: 978-1-936332-30-4 • $14.95

Voodoo in My Blood

A Healer's Journey from Surgeon to Shaman

Carolle Jean-Murat, M.D.

Born and raised in Haiti to a family of healers, US trained physician Carolle Jean-Murat came to be regarded as a world-class surgeon. But her success harbored a secret: in the operating room, she could quickly intuit the root cause of her patient's illness, often times knowing she could help the patient without surgery. Carolle knew that to fellow surgeons, her intuition was best left unmentioned. But when the devastating earthquake hit Haiti and Carolle returned to help, she had to acknowledge the shaman she had become.

"This fascinating memoir sheds light on the importance of asking yourself, 'Have I created for myself the life I've meant to live?'"
—**Christiane Northrup, M.D., author of the New York Times bestsellers:** *Women's Bodies, Women's Wisdom* **and** *The Wisdom of Menopause*

ISBN: 978-1-936332-05-2 • ePub: 978-1-936332-04-5 • $21.95

Fastest Man in the World

The Tony Volpentest Story

Tony Volpentest

Foreword by Ross Perot

Tony Volpentest, a four-time Paralympic gold medalist and five-time world champion sprinter, is a 2012 nominee for the Olympic Hall of Fame

"This inspiring story is about the thrill of victory to be sure—winning gold—but it is also a reminder about human potential: the willingness to push ourselves beyond the ledge of our own imagination. A powerfully inspirational story."
—**Charlie Huebner, United States Olympic Committee**

"This is a moving, motivating and inspiring book."
—**Dan O'Brien, world and Olympic champion decathlete**

"Tony's story shows us that no matter where we start the race, no matter what the obstacles, we all have it within us to reach powerful goals."
—**Oscar Pistorius, "Blade Runner," double amputee, world record holder in the 100, 200 and 400 meters**

ISBN: 978-1-936332-00-7 • ePub: 978-1-936332-01-4 • $16.95

MR. JOE

Tales from a Haunted Life

Joseph Barnett and Jane Congdon

Do you believe in ghosts? Nor did Joseph Barnett until the winter he was fired from his career job and became a school custodian to make ends meet. The fact that the eighty-five-year-old school where he now worked was built near a cemetery had barely registered with Joe when he was assigned the graveyard shift. But soon, walking the dim halls alone at night, listening to the wind howl outside, Joe was confronted with a series of bizarre and terrifying occurrences.

It wasn't just the ghosts of the graveyard shift that haunted him. Once the child of a distant father and an alcoholic mother, now a man devastated by a failed marriage, fearful of succeeding as a single dad, and challenged by an overwhelming illness, Joe is haunted by his own personal ghosts.

The story of Joseph's challenges and triumphs emerges as an eloquent metaphor of ghosts, past and present, real and emotional, and how a man puts his beliefs about self—and ghosts—to the test.

"Thrilling, thoughtful, elegantly told. So much more than a ghost story."
—**Cyrus Webb, CEO, Conversation Book Club**

"This is truly inspirational work, a very special book—a gift to any reader."
—**Diane Bruno, CISION Media**

ISBN: 978-1-936332-78-6 • ePub: 978-1-936332-79-3 • $18.95

Amazing Adventures of a Nobody

Leon Logothetis

From the Hit Television Series Aired in 100 Countries!

Tired of his disconnected life and uninspiring job, Leon Logothetis leaves it all behind—job, money, home, even his cell phone—and hits the road with nothing but the clothes on his back and five dollars in his pocket, relying on the kindness of strangers and the serendipity of the open road for his daily keep. Masterful storytelling!

"A gem of a book; endearing, engaging and inspiring."
—**Catharine Hamm, Los Angeles Times Travel Editor**

"Warm, funny, and entertaining. If you're looking to find meaning in this disconnected world of ours, this book contains many clues."   —**Psychology Today**

ISBN: 978-0-9843081-3-2 • ePub: 978-1-936332-51-9 • $14.95

The Search For
The Lost Army

The National Geographic and Harvard University Expedition

Gary S. Chafetz

In one of history's greatest ancient disasters, a Persian army of 50,000 soldiers was suffocated by a hurricane-force sandstorm in 525 BC in Egypt's Western Desert. No trace of this conquering army, hauling huge quantities of looted gold and silver, has ever surfaced.

Nearly 25 centuries later on October 6, 1981, Egyptian Military Intelligence, the CIA, and Israel's Mossad secretly orchestrated the assassination of President Anwar Sadat, hoping to prevent Egypt's descent—as had befallen Iran two years before—into the hands of Islamic zealots. Because he had made peace with Israel and therefore had become a marked man in Egypt and the Middle East, Sadat had to be sacrificed to preserve the status quo.

These two distant events become intimately interwoven in the story of Alex Goodman, who defeats impossible obstacles as he leads a Harvard University/ National Geographic Society archaeological expedition into Egypt's Great Sand Sea in search of the Lost Army of Cambyses, the demons that haunt him, and the woman he loves. Based on a true story.

Gary Chafetz, referred to as "one of the ten best journalists of the past twenty-five years," is a former Boston Globe correspondent and was twice nominated for a Pulitzer Prize by the Globe.

ISBN: 978-1-936332-98-4 • ePub: 978-1-936332-99-1 • $19.95

Bettie Youngs Books

We specialize in MEMOIRS

. . . books that celebrate fascinating people and remarkable journeys

In bookstores everywhere, online, Espresso, or from the publisher, Bettie Youngs Books
VISIT OUR WEBSITE AT
www.BettieYoungsBooks.com
To contact:
info@BettieYoungsBooks.com

www.ingramcontent.com/pod-product-compliance
Lightning Source LLC
Chambersburg PA
CBHW031309060426
42444CB00032B/901